I Don't Look Like What I Went Through, I'm Much Better

Tanicka Williams

I Don't Look What I Went Through, I'm Much Better

Copyright © 2020 by Tanicka Williams

ISBN: 978-1-7363436-0-9

Edited by Yulanda Henderson

Cover Design by Drake Creative

Printed in the United States of America

All rights reserved under the International Copyright Law. Contents and/or cover may not be reproduced in whole or in part in any form without the express written consent of the Publisher.

The names of the characters in this book has been changed to protect the innocent and identity of each person.

Table of Contents

Introduction 5

My Training into Being a Woman 7

Who Am I Really? 16

Close My Mouth: Open My Eyes 26

My Approach to Living a Better Life 36

Keeping My Sanity: Starting with Peace 43

Believe It or Not: I Do Matter 51

Introduction

To my wonderful gifts: Maurice, Mamadou, and Miisaun.

Always remember to aim for progression, not perfection! Shoot for the moon and you will land among the stars above.

Great growth doesn't come into your life through mountaintop experiences.

Great growth comes through the valleys and low places where you feel limited and vulnerable.

Remember all the things that I've taught you; you are kings, wise, intelligent, bold, strong, courageous, enduring, resilient, and young men of purpose.

Let love in and most of all, "BE" the love you want and need in your life.

-Mom

Chapter 1

My Training into Being a Woman

Before I even knew how to be someone's mother, I had to become a woman first. What exactly is a woman? To me being a woman meant that I was old enough to do the things that I wanted to do. I thought for a long time that I was old enough to do what I wanted only because I didn't have my mother there training or encouraging me on female etiquette, manners, respect for self as well as others, or having high esteem for myself.

I figured that once I turned 18 years old that I was grown enough to do womanly activities. Not fully understanding what it entails to be an adult, I took it upon myself to engage in worldly activities that I shouldn't have but thought it was fun and wouldn't hinder me in my maturity process.

Let's talk about maturity for a minute: being responsible, having common sense, being levelheaded and knowing how to conduct one's self. Can I just say, indulging in extracurricular activities such as: smoking, drinking, and being sexually active at my age is what I thought womanhood was all about. Honestly speaking, there was nothing responsible about putting substances into my body that were poisoning not only my body but also my mind.

At this point in my life, what I was doing felt good, but in all reality, I was starting to lose control of this so-called woman I was trying to become sooner than expected. After doing it for so long, I didn't know, nor did I care to see the person staring back at me in the mirror. How could I say that I was an adult when I didn't know who the person was staring back at me in the mirror?

Proverbs 27:19 (GNB) states, "It is your face that you see reflected in the water and it is your own self that you see in your heart". The sad part is what I was doing in my actions wasn't who I wanted to be in reality.

There was no one to blame when it came to my life because I was my own person at the end of the day, and no one could force me to do the things I considered right for me at the moment. There were times when I felt lonely, lacked morals, felt as though I'd lost my way, emotionally drained, and having a spiritual disconnect from God. Feeling this way only made me dive deeper into those evils I thought were coping mechanisms to fill the void of not having my parents not being a part of my life the way I wanted them to be.

There was no justification for my behavior at this particular time: except I was replacing one evil for another due to the fact I felt alone in my effort to be a productive part of society. Only sinking deeper in the pit, I was already in. Just because I couldn't admit my hurts, disappointments and feelings to others didn't mean that God had abandoned me.

1 Kings 8:57 (NLT) says, "May the LORD our God be with us, as he was with our ancestors; may he never leave us or abandon us." Even knowing this, I still decided I would live my life the way I wanted and when I messed up, all I had to do was tell God that I apologize. How many times do you think I went to Christ? I stopped counting after a while because I realized that I wasn't the person He would have me to be. How could I talk about being a woman when I was a filthy rag? I was dirty, thinking I was

clean, ignorant to the facts of life: having self-respect, carrying myself in a womanly manner, keeping myself safe for the man that deserved me, staying drug-free and that my words were either going to hinder or help someone else.

Usually, a person knows when they are doing wrong or hurting others because friends and even family start fading away. No one wanted to know about my problems and issues, so I kept everything I was feeling inside. I had become good at putting on a facade to make it seem as though everything was under control. What do I mean by control? Having the power to influence or direct my behavior or the course of my events. Thinking that I was in control of what I was doing hindered me, keeping me content with how I was living my life. I didn't stop to realize that my life wasn't my own at that time, but I thought I was grown, and I did what I wanted, how I wanted, with whomever I wanted to.

I didn't want to admit that everything I was doing was making me older than I was, making me tired, and keeping me from being successful in life. The Bible speaks upon, "Train up a child in the way they are to go: and when he is old, he will not depart from it" Proverbs 22:6 (KJV). When I read this, I thought the author was talking about parents teaching their children about being adults, but what I failed to see was that God wanted me to acknowledge Him despite of what I was doing. Proverbs 3:12 (GNB), "The LORD corrects those he loves, as parents correct a child of whom they are proud". I didn't want God's correction because then I would have to face myself in the mirror of reality and see that my actions would play a role in the woman I was supposed to be turning into or thought I was already.

Believe me when I tell you there is a difference between contentment and self-acceptance. Where I was in my life was being content with how I was living from day to day. To me there was nothing wrong in the relationships I had with men who were emotionally unavailable, going out often meeting people, nothing wrong with having a drink just so I could enjoy my time out. People often fall into the habit of doing things in routine that they don't see as being wrong or non-beneficial to their lives.

The truth of the matter is there is a difference between needing and wanting a person, thing, or particular place in your life. In thinking that we so-called need people, places, and things we engage in unnecessary activities that destroy us emotionally, physically, and more importantly psychologically. What is insanity? Doing the same thing and expecting a different result. How many people lose themselves (go insane) constantly volunteering themselves for the same activities, looking for a different outcome? How many times are we in denial about the wrong in the activities we engage in because if we admit it we would have to change ourselves? Being creatures of habit, a lot of times people don't see how the decisions we make affect those around us. Allowing myself to fall victim to the pressures of this world only hindered me without my knowledge. What I didn't realize at the time was that life for me became stagnant. I was stuck in my mess, but I was too far gone to see it. For me to have been settled with the way I was living meant that I had become comfortable with the people I was with, the activities I was engaging in, and having no regard for the consequences that I may have to face later on.

Can I talk about growing up quickly for a minute? I still remember this day as though it were yesterday: what was supposed to be a regular day turned into a nightmare for my family and a great realization for me. In dealing with my grandmother's passing, being the only one in the house working, and making sure my brother and sister were stable in all areas was stressful, but another step in pushing me to grow up before I was ready to. Dealing with the tsunami of responsibility so soon and not being adequately trained on how to be the best woman I could for those around me, I cried silently for many days and nights. I searched high and low to find that attachment to feeling secure, complete, and satisfied with my life. In the midst of endless activity, the monotony of life was setting in and every day I would ask what my purpose was here on earth. Was I being the best woman that I could be despite how I was living my life? Physically I was an adult, but mentally I was a little girl crying out to be seen and loved. Was I handling all my obligations correctly that were associated with being a woman?

There were two choices either have God guide my steps in His will or my own will. Job 14:16 (NKJV) tells us that "For now You number my steps" God numbers our steps" and Job 31:4 (NKJV) says, "Does He not see my ways, And count all my steps?" "He counts all our steps" and Job 34:21 (NKJV) "For His eyes are on the ways of man, And He sees all his steps." So, God numbers and counts our step; sees our entire goings and completes the void, the emptiness of the lives of his people.

In the training of becoming a woman many steps needed to be taken, so I could be the diamond that would shine brightly every day. I first had to understand that I wasn't alone in my journey to adulthood. Secondly, I was going to fail, fall, and have some bumps along the road. In falling, I had to dust myself off and not only try again but find a different way of doing things. In finding another way, I had to make sure that option B would be beneficial for my future. Also, in failing, I could ask questions to get the correct answers to make better choices and decisions.

The best part about asking questions was there weren't any wrong questions, nor there wasn't a single question I could ask God that He wouldn't answer. I failed to realize before, in handling things, that either I didn't ask God any questions or I didn't wait patiently for the answers. I didn't quite understand why my life was complacent, but now I realized it was because I wasn't allowing God to be the head in my heart, mind, and spirit.

I would say that I loved Christ, but I wasn't following the rules that came with allowing God's favor to be upon me. How could I set an example for anyone when my life was spiraling out of control right before my eyes and I did nothing to change it? I would be the first to call myself a woman without really understanding what that meant.

Usually, when you're training for something there's a coach to help you be the best in your craft, but that wasn't so in my case. In my training, I had failures, upsets, unhealthy relationships, disappointments, and being weary at times. Also, in training you have to be mentally prepared for that particular event coming up, but I wasn't sure what it was I was facing, so I didn't prepare causing me to fail and fall again.

In my training, I learned that I was going to have some lonely times and feel as though I was in it by myself. Believe it or not there was a small noticeable difference between being alone and having loneliness. To be alone was to be by myself, on the other hand, to be lonely was to suffer the feelings of loneliness, to want people, social contact, and yet unable to feel fulfilled. How was I surrounded by people but felt so alone? How could I be crying out for help and no one hear me? How was it that for so long I made myself believe I was happy, but honestly, I was just accepting myself for the person I thought I had to be. What I didn't see in my training was that my audience was that person I didn't dare face in the mirror of reality.

Even though there were many steps into womanhood/adulthood that I should've taken heed to I couldn't bear the shame of admitting I was becoming the person I told myself I didn't want to be. Someone told me that a fool learns from his own mistakes, but a wise man learns from the mistakes of others. It takes great responsibility to admit when I was wrong, but I took every day as a lesson learned. For a good while, I was a fool only because I was ignorant to correction and the possibility of change. How could I be beneficial to anyone when I was drowning in the pool of misery myself? How would my future look if I didn't quit running in the fast track instead of getting in the slow lane?

While going down the fast track I couldn't see that God had a plan for my life. Do you know how events went wrong in my life because I didn't follow the instructions of life? Psalm 119:175 (GNT) says, "Give me life, so that I may praise you; may your instructions help me". With this being said, I wasn't being obedient to what I should've been doing: LISTENING and OBEYING the will of God.

Accountability and responsibility will shape all people into the kind of person they need to be for the tomorrows of their lives.

Chapter 2

Who Am I Really?

"Who am I really?" is a question that could be asked for so many reasons because every day I struggled to identify myself with a particular category of female. However, I didn't know that females were put into one group; I was just trying to be me! Do you know there were plenty of times where I didn't think highly of myself or anything else at all?

When I was younger, I never thought I was pretty because all I ever heard was my sister was the pretty one; she had nice skin, long fine hair, and was lighter than I. Also, having people question whether we had the same parents wasn't exactly fun for me. How was I supposed to feel when no one around me looked like me, including my brother and sister? You can only imagine how low I would feel at times or how much I did everything to reinvent myself to fit in with what people called "normal". How ironic was it that at 12 years old I was making myself look like everyone else when at this age people were supposed to be accepting me for me or so I thought. It didn't help that I didn't have a female figure helping or coaching me along so I could know what or what not to do in my transformation from little girl to teenager. Even when I felt as though I got it right there were snickers from people, questions still being asked, and no one telling me that I was fine just the way I was.

Being in a home where my sister was concerned about herself, having an absentee mother, and making sure my brother was good took a lot of work, but this shaped my thinking towards others instead of myself.

From what I can remember, from about 10-15 years old, I didn't quite fit into any fashion trend at school or around the way. It wasn't until I started working part-time at the age of 16 and entering my junior year of high school that I decided I needed a drastic change. After realizing I didn't have to fit into anyone else's idea of what I needed to look like, I made my own look.

After a while, I was starting to get noticed for being different than everyone around me. At this moment, my viewpoint of myself changed externally, my self-esteem grew more, and I realized that no one's opinion of me mattered anymore. Walking with new confidence meant that I didn't care about what others thought of Sharese Conners. At this point in my high school career, I was no longer Kristen's sister because honestly up to my junior year no one even knew that we were related.

After a while, I accepted that I had to step out of the shadows and make my presence known, not just in school but for the rest of my life. Where was I going to start? Being that senior year was soon approaching I abused the three months I had to reinvent myself. Soon coming to the beginning year, I knew that things were going to be looking up for me because, not only did I change my appearance, but I was working so I was independent of myself.

Who knew that reinventing myself would become a full-time job? I was starting to have a different outlook on the person I wanted to be. I was starting to become this sophisticated young lady who was able to express herself openly. At this time, I was more aware of what I liked and didn't like, how to budget my money, and who I was becoming. I didn't even realize that I was evolving into the butterfly that I was to become. This was the beginning of the strain between my sister and me. It seemed the more successful I was becoming, the further she distanced herself from me. What was going on that my sister didn't want to be friends with me? I couldn't explain it, so eventually I let it go and continued to prosper on with my life because I wanted to make sure my brother was okay, go to school, work and still make it in life.

Being in a house where the people around are physically there yet far away can take a toll on one's spirit. My grandmother was the glue that held 268 Harrison Street together with her love, dedication to people, and patience with children who didn't belong to her. I loved my grandmother because in the years of trying to figure out who I was she always let me know that despite the situation I was special, and I was going to be great at everything I attempted to conquer. I started telling myself that despite my mother and father's absence, I refused to be known as Carol's daughter or Jay and Kristen's sister, so I started living my life as though my family wasn't torn apart.

No one ever knew that my home was broken, dysfunctional, and not exactly your conventional living situation. How was I doing all that I was doing without realizing how hurt or tired I was becoming? Why didn't anyone ever ask me if I was alright? How was it that I wasn't the oldest but played the role of the oldest child, mother, father, and caretaker to so many people except myself? Was this my reality? Despite everything and wanting better for myself, I managed to set my priorities straight by staying focused on school, maintaining good grades, juggling work, assisting in the house's responsibilities, and doing the right thing because this was expected of me (the invisible sister). It's funny how I used to refer to myself as the invisible sister only because for so long no one saw me. I would often ask myself, "Where did I stand?" because I didn't have the beauty of my sister or the athleticism of my brother, but I refused to continue to be overlooked.

    I was in an environment that I really didn't want to be in and made it my business to save my money to eventually move out. Trusting that moving back to East Orange was going to happen, I allowed someone to fool me into giving them my money to find me a place that didn't exist. Disappointed, frustrated, and mad I still had to press forward, so I made it my mission to save everything I had for a place of my own that I deserved. When making my plans, I never factored in meeting someone who would become my partner in life. I'll never forget the day I met this stunning; man, who I decided would be mine—not questioning whether he was right for me. I asked Mohummad out on a date. Still unsure what I was looking for or where we might go, I pursued him not expecting anything except for him to want to be with me.

    After dating him for a couple of months, I learned that I was pregnant and this is when our lives together began. I still had no idea of what would happen with us, but I trusted that he was willing to do the right thing by this life we created together. My life would never be the same again, having this man in it showing me what true love was supposed to look like. After realizing I didn't want to be his "Baby mama," I asked him to marry me and he genuinely said yes.

After only being engaged for a brief time on July 10, 2006, I became Mrs. Washington, not just his wife, but a partner in life. Still having doubts, I did my very best to make sure my family was being taken care of by working every day, taking care of our son, and respecting my husband as being the head of the household. Due to my lack of experience in being in a relationship clouded my judgment of whether I was enough for him. I wasn't sure if he was happy with being my husband or doing it because we were already living together and had a son. Don't get me wrong, I loved him, but the flesh side of me would wonder if I was what he wanted. Even with feeling this way, I still honored and respected him because I wanted us to have an effective marriage. Yes, I would get worried, but I couldn't let that consume my thinking because then I would get mad at what I thought could happen when he wasn't around me. For the next few months, our marriage flourished that we lived on Fairview Avenue while raising our son and letting each other into the other's personal space from time to time. Being a mother and wife for the first time came with unexpected changes, but I was up for the journey that came with both roles.

After being in our first apartment with my husband and son changed my viewpoint of the kind of person I was becoming. I was taking joy in my roles of being a mother, a wife, and now a respectable woman. It wasn't going to happen overnight, but eventually I was going to have to grow up and take responsibility for anything good, bad, and indifferent concerning my immediate family. Did I know what I was doing when it came to my son? Hell no! What about being married? I had no idea what I was supposed to be doing; there wasn't a manual for what I threw myself into, but I had to trust that I could make correct decisions concerning them both. The kind of relationship that he and I were developing was stable and consistent with family business, so I had no problem with the way my house was being run.

He would work hard to make sure that our son and the house was taken care of, staying extra hours at work and attempting to find another job. Still trusting him to provide the house's finances, I made sure that I kept the household duties done. Were we husband and wife? Partners in life? Co-parents to our son? Were we doing things because they were protocol? At this point were we happy anymore? Settling for the way things were going? Was this love or a living situation? Were we comfortable with one another and what we had? I would wonder even more at this point because for a good while I felt as though we were going through the motions of maintaining a household. In December 2006, maintaining our home took a tragic turn when we lost our house to an electrical fire.

After leaving our house in the morning, where everything seemed to be in order, we came back only to see that everything we owned was gone! Feeling afraid, distraught, sad, hurt, and unsure where we were going to live, I couldn't do anything but cry at this time. Being my support system, he consoled me and told me that everything was going to be alright. Showing me that we were in this situation together reassured me that he was in it for the long haul, not just for me, but for our family. That night we stayed with his family, but after thinking about it we agreed that it would be beneficial to stay with my aunt and uncle. The hurtful part of staying with them was that my son couldn't stay with us and he had to live temporarily with his grandmother.

This put me in a depressed state because I didn't have my son, my living situation was back to square one, and my marriage was shifting due to the space we were in. I can't speak for my husband, but I knew that this was a change neither one of us liked but accepted until we found something better. At that point, I didn't care about a place; I just wanted my son with me every day where I could touch him, see his face, and make sure that he was alright.

Being grateful to my family for their hospitality, I had to mask the pain I felt every day without my son. As time went forward, I felt a disconnect from my partner, husband, baby father, etc... A woman can pick up on when her man is changing up his routine, especially when it's not geared towards her. When we moved into my aunt's house it was Christmas season, so I was excited about spending this time with my family, having Devon with us and being happy. Little did I know that this was the beginning of the swinging doors my husband let people (women) walk through. Why would his co-worker be getting him gifts knowing he had a wife at home? What was being said for her to think it acceptable to give a married man anything?

How did he think I would feel finding out about this? What was I supposed to do or say about the idea of my husband cheating on me? Was I to leave him? Do I confront him? Every emotion ran through my mind at this point: only not to get any answers, so I left it alone because I didn't know how to interact with him at this time.

I decided I didn't want my family to split over my assumptions, so I didn't say anything about the red flags being waved in my face. How was I going to explain to my family that I was separating from my husband; that my marriage was failing? Unable to wrap my mind around the thought, I continued to be the supportive wife and soon to be mother of another son.

Sometime after finding out that we were pregnant again we found an apartment and I thought my marriage would have a turning point. We were on our own again and communication was increasing. I was hopeful that we would be good. I guess asking for a happy marriage was too much! Nothing is worse than having someone tell you that your partner tried to get with them; this is not what a wife wants to hear being six months pregnant. This was a nightmare and I just wanted to wake up from the misery. My life; tragic but true and I knew I deserved so much more. Still not showing any emotion towards him because I needed to be strong for my boys. I stayed silent. All I needed from him was love, respect, loyalty, and effective communication, but this was hard for him. What was I supposed to do now that my partner was uninterested? Not saying that I was completely innocent in my marriage after dealing with my husband's infidelity, but honestly speaking, what does one do in a dead marriage?

Chapter 3

Close My Mouth: Open My Eyes

As my marriage progressed, I realized that even though he was my husband, he was becoming more so my roommate; sleeping in the same bed, having sex, and being responsible for the continued bills in our shared living space was starting to be protocol instead of enjoyment. Why was this happening to us? I came to the conclusion that the love left when he did, only it was too late for me to see it at that given time.

What exactly was too late you ask? Finding condoms in his pockets, him coming in from work only to go back out after telling me that he'd be tired, or not forthcoming about whom he would be going out with. All the signs of him wanting to be single were there, so I just closed my mouth and opened my eyes to what was taking place in my home.

You couldn't tell me that I wasn't "Inspector Gadget" because every opportunity I had I was checking pockets, going through his phones, asking questions, and being observant of the changes in his behavior.

Yes, I played the jealous wife role because my so-called husband stopped being my husband and became someone I didn't know anymore. Was what I was doing fair to him? Probably not, but what he was doing wasn't fair either, so I just wanted to know who I was sleeping with every night. After a while, I stopped the detective work and started keeping to myself; woman code. I started living as though I was single as well.

At this point in my relationship, no one could tell me that I wasn't single because for about four years there was no monogamy from him; just me trying to hold on for the sake of the children.

What was on my mind at the starting point of my newfound singleness? Did I have an objective of what I was going to do? After getting hit by the waves of ups and downs in my marriage, I started to embrace myself more and cherish the fact that I was going to be giving birth to our second son Gil on Sept. 10, 2007. Would adding another baby to the family help us? Would the strain of caring for two children overwhelm either one of us? How long before one of us would fold under pressure from putting up a sham for so long? What was it going to take for my so-called marriage to get back on track? How sad was it that I was married, but my husband left me long before we decided to officially divorce? Who was I kidding? I knew that I wasn't strong enough to move on and I didn't want to create a wedge between my boys and him, so I decided that my marriage was worth saving and I needed my best friend back.

In doing so, I maintained a healthy level of respect, open communication and loved him despite everything I felt was lacking with us. Still, no one knew how lonely I felt, how sad I was becoming, or angry that my husband was giving his attention to someone else. Why did I have to compete with the side chick? What was she doing that I wasn't? Still not mentioning that I managed to stay faithful to a man that was living a single life.

Being the woman, I had to make sure that my children never saw what was going on with us, so I would pretend for a long time that daddy was around and that my boys weren't affected by his absences. What was I going to do at this point of him not being around? I wasn't going to allow my boys to see me hurt, crying, and neglected, so I picked up the pieces of my life and stayed in my lane... I was a wife and mother, period!

There wasn't anything that anyone could say that would change my mind of feeling as though I was a single mother. He might've been in the home, but he wasn't supporting my children or me as the man of the house. Not saying that he wasn't attempting, but from when we first met to our second son's birth, he started paying attention to unnecessary people, places, and things. For a good while, I thought like this... LOVE CONQUERED ALL.

Not knowing what to expect from me stepping out of my marriage, I continued to keep my mouth closed about either one of our actions. But I kept my eyes open so I could see and understand that this wasn't normal nor did it feel good, but it was necessary at the time. What I failed to see was that by me indulging in the act of adultery I wasn't doing any better than he was. How could I look in the mirror and accept the person staring back at me when I didn't know who she was? At this point, I was creating another problem that I would have to get myself out of.

For a long time, I was living a double life; pretending to be the devoted wife, mother of two boys at this time, and a good homemaker when honestly, I was not behaving as a mother, wife, or a woman who respected herself. Not looking at the consequences to follow, I continued to meet people, have secret affairs, and keep my mouth shut about my open marriage.

Laughing to mask the hurt I was going through knowing that my home was broken and neither he nor I was doing anything to put the pieces back together. Every day we were together seemed more unreal because I believed both of us realized our marriage was ending; however, neither of us wanted to say the words aloud. Divorce was the resolution to the problem that was our failed marriage. Who gets married only to get divorced? Certainly not I, but I wasn't happy with him as my partner/provider and he stopped seeing me as his wife. I'd rather be comfortable by myself than miserable with someone that decided I wasn't enough for them.

Let's not forget my best friend named "Temptation" he came 6'7", chiseled back, dark chocolate, and treated me as though I was the only woman around. I allowed myself to give in to my craving, which was this man that I thought came at the right time. What I thought was the right time was and that maybe the grass was greener on the other side.

The summer of 2009 was the beginning of my secret relationship that stemmed from a quick meet, sexual relations, and endless phone conversations and text messages. Who would've thought that my happiness would have come while still in my marriage? This probably sounds weird and wrong, but these relationships are more common than people realize. Thinking about it, I wanted to be happy. Was I a bad woman for having another relationship?

If I told my husband what I'd done, would he be upset? Would he come clean about his infidelity? Could we possibly be honest and maybe talked about reconciliation? Many thoughts ran through my mind when the odds were stacked up against me.

I decided to deal with what I was facing and suffer the consequences later. Still enjoying the excitement of having someone pay attention to me I decided to continue to give in to my temptation of another man. Not wanting to draw attention to myself, I closed my mouth about the inconsistency in my husband's behavior and kept my eyes open on my behavior because now I was aware of what was happening but didn't necessarily care anymore. At this time, I was being honest with myself; integrity was telling me the truth and honesty was telling the truth to other people.

As a woman, it was only a matter of time before I was going to have to take another look in my mirror of self-reflection and ask: who are you? Was I happy with the person looking back at me? I was mindful that my behavior wasn't adding up to what I portrayed to others.

My thought process was changing regarding myself, my marriage, and the relationships I had with people. Yes, even though my marriage was a phony at this point, I still longed for those moments where maybe we could've talked about where we went wrong, where both of us stopped caring about the other person's needs, wants, and feelings. No one ever told me that marriage would be easy, and I knew it wasn't going to be, but how did we get to the point of carelessness? Was love even still being offered anymore? Was respect a factor of reconciliation? How was I going to juggle my lifestyle: husband, secret lover, and maintain my household? Something on this list had to be adjusted so I could have order, peace, and some sort of stability in my life.

When I thought about what I was doing it came to a point of good or bad, right or wrong in the sense of what was beneficial to my sanity and the symbol of commitment. I started to understand that I didn't have the energy for my marriage and was secretly sneaking around with another man. How could I explain what I was doing to anyone who found out? What I was doing felt good but was bad in the eyes of God because no matter what was being done, two wrongs didn't make a right. Being a mother, I wasn't setting a good example of respect for my boys; as a woman, I wasn't respecting myself, and I was in denial about my behavior. There are three choices I could make; give up, give in or give it your all.

As much as I thought I was happy with what I was doing, I actually wasn't content with myself, I felt there was more for me, but I couldn't quite understand what "that more" was. Was I allowing myself to settle for this mediocre life? Why wasn't I striving for better for the sake of my family? I trusted that having a husband and a family was enough as long as both of us worked on making sure our relationship was solid and had a stable foundation. Even after stopping what I was doing outside the home, I still felt as though I wasn't living up to my full potential.

Going to work every day, cooking, cleaning, and submitting to a man that didn't appreciate me was another obstacle in itself because I had to keep this facade up for so long. Why couldn't both of us communicate the flaws, shortcomings, and missing pieces of our marriage to one another? What happened from the time we got married until we had our now third son Abdul on Sept. 10, 2010? Was I ever enough for him? Did he ever really love me? When I asked him to marry me, did he really want to or did he just want it for his convenience? Believing that love conquered all, I accepted the actions taken in my household.

After a while, I stopped asking questions and opened my eyes to the fact that I just might have to live life without him. This was difficult to think about, but it became a reality whenever I would sleep alone, take my boys to work with me, and get no explanation of where my husband might've been the night before. I'm not sure how long this went on, but I knew I was tired of crying, being hurt by him, and feeling neglected when I tried my best to make my house my home.

What exactly was happiness? Was I truly happy or was I going according to what the Bible said I was supposed to do? I was supposed to love, honor, and cherish my husband till death do us part, right? Where in those vows did it say: love, honor, and cherish till we get tired of one another?

Realistically this is what happened in my marriage because we both succumb to the pressures of this world. Once we knew that separation was the only solution, we respected one another's decision to dissolve the marriage. This way, both parties could have peace and still respect the other person.

Now that dissolution was the only option, how would I explain their father's absence in the home? What could either one of us have done to solidify our relationship? Were we supposed to be married or did I just not want to be his baby mama? Would we be happier without one another now? Would my boys feel as though it was their fault because he was gone? How were we going to interact now that we were divorced? What people don't understand is being divorced takes on another job as well because now visitation, schedules adjusted, finances discussed, and different emotions play out. Who wants to get married to get divorced; when divorce happens, both parties need not feel any way against the other person because the majority of the time there are children involved?

Respect... is the appreciation of the separation of the person, of the ways in which he or she is unique. Even the divorce has made me appreciate my ex-husband because in going through this, my experience of being with him helped me to understand what I need and want in my next marriage. It sounds funny that I want to get married again, but God has allowed me to unharden my heart to allow love in again with understanding, acceptance, and patience for my partner. Also, being in a relationship where I separated myself, I realized that all things take work, and I know now that if I want the best for my husband, I have to give of myself because I'm a better woman for choosing to have a relationship with God for myself.

Being in a relationship without allowing God to be the third strand in our braid was part of the reason that things didn't work between him and me. It wasn't a lack of love, but a lack of friendship that made us not be completely naked with one another. I could talk about how fun it was, but honestly speaking, were we best friends? Did he see me as someone that he could express himself honestly and openly to? Now that I think about it, how many times did we enjoy one another's company without the boys? How could we live together but didn't communicate daily with each other?

Thinking about my marriage opens my mind to the possibility of tomorrow's blessings. The hand of God moving on my behalf: shifting me from where I was to a place of comfortability. I'm no longer angry, disappointed, or frustrated about what went wrong. I'm in a good place because I understand that even when we cause an action, God allows there to be a reaction so that we could either be blessed, be a blessing, or be comfortable enough, so He could move us from that place to where we need to be.

Chapter 4
My Approach to Living a Better Life

So, I moved from Monticello, in August 2012, to a friend's house for a little while until I moved into my apartment in November. Congrats to me on taking the first step of what I considered independence. Having my own apartment, being divorced, and living life as a single mother came as a ripple effect all at once and this was something I was going to have to accept.

When I first moved into my apartment, I was uncomfortable because I lived with other people for so long and was accustomed to dealing with different personalities. In celebrating my newfound independence, I started having get-togethers regularly on Friday and Saturday nights that lasted well into the morning hours: not realizing what kind of impression this would have on those I had around me. Also, not considering what negative effect this might have on my children, I welcomed people openly into my home for drinks, conversation, entertainment, and always a great time. What was becoming of my behavior? Was this how I wanted to live my life as an independent woman? What impression was I setting for my boys? How did people coming to my get-togethers view me? I didn't know at the time that just because I was living on my own didn't mean that I was independent or responsible.

I believe we are solely responsible for the choices we make, and we must accept the consequences of every deed, word, and thought that turns into action in our lives. Honestly speaking, every action had a reaction and I didn't think it would affect my future or my children. Even when my thought process didn't factor in what would or could happen later; I was existing instead of living a comfortable lifestyle. Some people would probably ask what a comfortable life for me would've been. The word comfortable means being in a state of physical or mental comfort, contented, and at ease. Was I at ease in my house at the time? With my life? Dealing with my newfound independence took some time getting used to, but if I wanted to set an example, I would have to start thinking differently for the boys.

I surrounded myself with positive people showing them that better was right in front of them. Now I'm not saying that it was easy; there were some hills to climb and some people had to be cut off in order for me to move forward. Having unhealthy relationships, maintaining my independence, raising my boys as a single mother, and juggling a full load was havoc at times to deal with, but I made it work. As a woman, single mother, and working full time, I didn't understand why I didn't allow myself a break once in a while. Would I have been wrong if I would've taken a couple of days off to get my thought process together? I wanted a small vacation for maybe a week or two. When was it going to be my turn to just get away for a while without interruption? Yes, I had my own place, but was I truly happy or satisfied with the way things were turning out?

Having company almost every day throughout the week was fun, but not conducive or beneficial in my process to be a productive part of society. Not being in any fulfilling relationships wasn't exactly helping my current state of mind either. Not that my boys were asking questions, but I felt they knew what was going on and but didn't quite understand any of it. How was I going to attempt to give them an explanation when I was losing all sense of what reality was myself?

I knew that I must be "well" even to attempt to explain or comprehend for myself what was going on. But when was I going to get my "wellness"? I started living a more structured lifestyle, not only for myself but also for my children. My wellness approach to better health was adopting a variety of healthy habits for full functioning on all levels, such as: mental, physical, social, and spiritual. This approach is different because I thought that health was merely the absence of pain or symptoms but learned wellness was a view of health that emphasized the state of the entire being and its ongoing development. I viewed wellness as an interactive process of becoming aware of and practicing healthy choices to create a more successful and balanced lifestyle.

Physically I wasn't in the best shape to be active with my boys. Mentally I didn't always make the best decisions for the sake of my household. Socially, I allowed myself to be surrounded by negativity with those people, places, and things that weren't always productive for me. I can't forget my spirituality that was gradually dwindling only because I wasn't allowing God to be the head of my life. I wasn't living a life according to his will, nor did I see his hand moving on my behalf. How was I going to live a healthy lifestyle without the commonsense given to me, without having a relationship with Christ, not teaching my children how to be gentlemen, and losing myself in the circus I called my life?

The way I gave of myself to others was a measure of how much I respected and liked myself. However, while entertaining people, I was losing myself, not realizing it at the time because I would have had to look in the mirror and face the person staring back at me. Who wants to admit that what they're doing is wrong? Who can honestly say that while in the moment they say, "I can't do this!" "I need to stop this!!!" All people fall short because we live in the flesh and we mess up DAILY! It's not the fall we need to worry about, but what happens after we get up that makes the difference. As a mother and someone who wanted Christ, I had to think about what I was going to do when I got up. Was I going to turn from those people, places, and things that I allowed to pull me down so low that I couldn't see the upside or a way out?

It was time for me to get my house in order starting with my thought process: meaning I had to reintroduce myself to Christ all over again because at this point, I didn't know him for me. Secondly, I had to get a made-up mind that I didn't have to surround myself with negative people, places, and things anymore. Thirdly, the environment around me wasn't beneficial to my children, so I had to figure out how I was going to get from Ocean Avenue quickly. There had to be changes made so everything in my life could start falling into place the way they were supposed to. I knew that it was going to take time and effort, but I was prayerful that Christ would bring my children and me out.

Just because I was of age didn't mean I was near the place I needed to be mentally, spiritually, emotionally, nor physically to handle everything God needed for me to acquire in my life. Speaking of "my life," how could I have called it mine when I wasn't aware of the woman I was turning into because of the decisions I was making. I couldn't admit that my life was out of control and it was my fault.

The decisions I chose to make were wrong. The problem with me was all my life, whenever it came to decision making, I would make it and forget about it. What I mean when I say "forget about it" is, I would make my decision based upon what would be the best outcome for me at that moment. Before having my children, I never cared nor understood that my actions affected me now and later. As I got older and started having relationships with different people, I would see the effects and didn't appreciate the reactions. How could what I was doing be so terrible, especially since I was doing it in the privacy of my own home? What I failed to realize was that a home could be disrespected, but I didn't stop to think about that.

How could I ask people to respect me and my home if I was acting out of order? Not only wasn't I respecting my house, but no one in it as well and this was when I had to reevaluate my thinking. At this point in my life, I was compromising myself because I was indulging in activities that I knew were wrong, especially with children present in the home.

People would tell me that consistency was important especially if I wanted to see results. How was I going to see the type of results I needed if I wasn't willing to put forth the effort necessary for growth? Where was I going to start? What area of my life needed the most attention? What had become of me since moving into my own home? How did I allow myself to get caught up in the mayhem that I surrounded myself with? I had to start living a more productive beneficial life, not only for me but also for my children. Getting my house in order meant I had to separate myself from the outside distractions and focus more on having an intimate connection with Christ. I knew that I could become the woman I was born to be, but it was up to me to revitalize that fire within me yet again. It was pivotal that I changed for the sake of my children.

I desperately needed to get it together. I did just that and I didn't engage in those activities that I thought were fun for me at that particular time. No one told me that the road would be easy, but I found out how hard it was and still thought that I would be able to walk it. Little did I know, I didn't have on the right shoes for the journey, so my feet grew weary and I had some detours that rerouted me and took me off course. After changing my thought process, I had to redirect myself to see the right way so that travels wouldn't be too long to get where I wanted to be.

In redirecting myself, I lost friends, acquaintances, stopped smoking; I was not drinking as much and drew myself closer to my children. However, in doing all of this I wasn't taking care of my monetary responsibilities such as rent, so of course it came to either paying or leaving. As much as I wanted to stay in my apartment, all good things come to an end and in October 2013, I left Ocean Avenue.

Chapter 5

Keeping My Sanity: Starting with Peace

I believe that with every action comes a reaction and the reaction from not doing what I needed to do on Ocean caused me to have to move and in November 2013, I no longer resided in my old place anymore. I'm grateful for the move I had to make because this was an opportunity for me to gather my perspective of a better life for my boys and me. A friend was kind enough to allow the boys and me to stay with him until I could get on my feet again.

I didn't know how long it would take for me to get financially stable, but this was a start in the right direction. Not only did I move from where I used to live, but I was starting a new job as well. I saw that maybe there was hope for me yet, so I stayed the course of not smoking and drinking too much, so I could have a better relationship with those around me. I didn't want to uproot my boys from the school they were attending, so I adjusted to taking them via bus most days and then going to work. Yes, this was a major adjustment in my life, but any time I wanted something to be different I had to be willing to change myself.

Not knowing how this move was going to affect my boys, I knew that staying where I was wasn't going to be beneficial for any of us. Being that the boys were young, didn't know any better, or didn't have a say in the matter, I did what I thought would be in the best interest of all of us. At this point, I was prayerful that a change of scenery would refocus my thinking, help me build a relationship with the boys, and I was slowly grasping a sense of balance between work and leisure.

It was more than time that was needed for me to get back right with God. I was existing instead of living the life that was planned for me. It was going to take some work, but I was willing to challenge myself so that I could show my boys that with effort comes great reward. Don't get me wrong, not every day was easy, but I made strides to separate myself from those strongholds like alcohol, tobacco and sexual immoralities.

Once I moved in with my friend, I thought that I would be able to just pay my portion of the rent, stay out of his way, and continue to live my life, but this was harder than I thought. Not only was the physicality of things rough, having to give up my substance of choice: alcohol was hard because this was my coping mechanism to dealing with everyday life and the people in my circle. The hardest part about giving up the people, places, and things was that I wasn't sure if I was strong enough to go without having to have a drink in my system in order to enjoy my time outside the house. At this time, I knew my life was going downhill and I needed someone to reach out and grab me before I reached the very bottom.

I don't know how long it took, but I know it didn't happen overnight. As a matter of fact, putting one's life back together is a daily process that no one ever gets right. Even those who have never had to really deal with substance abuse can say they had it easy because there's no such thing when you're doing your best to stay on the right path. As a young mother and servant of God, I know firsthand that life will and can chew you up and spit you out. Many times, I wanted to give up, but there was a voice that would whisper to me, "You will be fine as long as you hold my hand."

Being in someone else's house took some getting used to, but it was my motivation not to go back to those activities that I thought I really enjoyed. Moving in with my friend was an eye-opener with me finding my worth; so, I slowly managed to cut off everyone that I felt wasn't beneficial to my process at this point. This wasn't the easiest task to overcome only because for a good while; I thought that everyone in my circle was my friend and I couldn't see how I was going to close the door on some of them. Many times, I couldn't understand that in order to be productive in society I had to be mentally stable enough to handle different relationships, work, and maintain a healthy lifestyle. For a length of time, I was working on the outside appearance while the inside was crumbling slowly; eventually, I had to make up my mind that it's not what I look like, but the renewing of my mind.

The question was always why; why some women choose to remain in unfulfilled meaningless relationships that don't serve a purpose? I was this woman, so I had to examine why I stayed in a marriage that eventually faded over the years. I didn't realize that my sons were watching the relationships I engaged in. It would be to the point that my partner and I would often use and abuse one another. As a result of this, we both became products and participants of broken relationships, years of psychological and emotional pain, unwanted baggage, dysfunction, and loss of respect for self and others.

Because I was freshly divorced and thought I could do what I wanted, I didn't notice that my decisions were causing damage, not only to me but also to my boys. Relationships are not as complicated as we make them out to be. At the end of the day, I believe it's all about LOVE! What I've come to realize at this stage in my life is that God is love. The purpose of life is to show the love that Christ has shown us.

Love strengthens us. It fosters greatness and motivates peace; however, there will be times where we will win and lose some of the battles we go through. I had to be the love that I wanted and needed in any relationship. Love isn't just what I do, but it's the actions I show, who I am, and what I need at that time. Speaking of what I needed; I started a relationship with my guy friend I was living with, so to me this was supposed to be a fresh start. However, we didn't exactly start off on a smooth note, but I was willing to give it a chance because I cared about him.

We would have conversations about our dreams, relationship, sex, and what we wanted from one another, so to me this seemed as though he wanted the best out of what we had going on. I didn't want to rock the boat, so I pretended that I was fine with him and what was talked about looked promising. I didn't know why I would have agreed to share him with another woman, but this is what I did to make him happy. I knew somewhere down the line things with us would always be rocky.

Things being "rocky" was an understatement between my partner and me only because I would get frustrated because I wasn't appreciated or valued. Why was I allowing this man to disrespect me by not valuing the time we were supposed to be spending together? Why was I allowing myself to be with someone that obviously didn't see how hurt I was feeling? Was I settling for him just because we lived together? Once again, I put myself in a situation where I thought our friendship would outweigh the relationship factor.

Sometimes I would want to end things, but who gives up on someone they love? Why would I break up with him when we lived together and shared the same space? Would it be awkward for us since we lived in the same house, having sexual relationships, and the responsibilities of the home? My children also had a relationship with him at this point due to him being there prior to us living together. He was treating my boys as though he knew them forever, so this made me overlook the fact that he and I weren't clicking anymore. On the flip side, there were moments that were good for us, but this didn't mean that I was happy. What would have made me happy was having someone who I knew had my best interest at heart, supporting me in all endeavors, and letting me know I mattered to them. Where was this attention I was supposed to get from him? Why did it always feel as though I had to suggest something to get what I was looking for? I understand that a real relationship takes communication, quality time, and acts of kindness, gifts, and physical touch.

Now, if a relationship is built on all these things, why did I always have to ask when it should've been offered without hesitation? It's hard being with someone who is happiest when they're not with you. Being introduced to people as the friend when I was the girlfriend, how was I supposed to feel about this? Was I supposed to stay in this so-called relationship or was it time to call it quits due to the blatant disrespect? Whether I wanted to work it out or let it go, we would still be roommates. The funny part about all of this was that I didn't even know why I decided to be in a relationship with someone I had to share.

A successful relationship isn't built on givers and takers, but that of people who share themselves. What exactly were we sharing other than the space we lived in? How could the relationship progress when it didn't feel as though I was being treated as the girlfriend first and roommate second? I allowed things between him and me to continue to find out maybe this wasn't what either one of us wanted. I didn't think that either one of us set out to get together and fall apart, but slowly this is what wound up happening.

Believing that things would change and we both would be satisfied with the other person, we started to tend to each other's needs in regard to spending more time, words of affirmation, and acts of kindness. Unfortunately, ungratefulness set in and we were back to square one. At this point, I started asking myself personal questions like: Do I deserve this treatment? Am I worthy of someone better? Why am I with him? Due to these unanswered questions, I needed to make a conscious decision that if I stayed things would have to change and if I decided to leave the relationship, could we salvage the friendship? I had to keep in mind that we lived together, so I didn't want it to be where he and I couldn't be civil with one another at any time in or out of the house.

Being mature about the situation meant that we needed to respect each other's feelings, how we spoke to one another, and the boundaries in the house. For months we went back and forth trying to figure out if what we felt was what both of us wanted; even though our mouths said yes, our hearts were far from that. I believed we cared about one another but didn't have any idea of what it would take to be in a committed relationship. Going through months of not saying too much, it was evident our relationship was over and in November 2014, we decided it was time to let things go.

Chapter 6
Believe It or Not: I Do Matter

Deciding to part ways from my ex was a decision I thought would've been easy on us, but it came with emotional baggage I didn't need. Yes, we are still living together, but he must've thought that this meant that he could still have boyfriend privileges. I'm an adult, so I can take responsibility for my part in the mess, but he actually thought that he could have his cake and eat it too. Didn't he know that once we broke up, I was no longer obligated to "DO" anything for him anymore? Yes, we all are human, have desires, urges, and needs, but there comes a time when you realize that how you treat people comes back to you.

Still not knowing my worth, I allowed myself to get caught up in the madness that was "OUR" so-called friendship. After a while, I realized that the state I was in wasn't healthy for anyone involved: myself, my children, nor him, only because I was getting to my breaking point and eventually someone would get hurt.

Forgiveness is not a choice; it is an obligation that I was willing to make for the sake of peace in the house I lived in with him. To truly forgive someone, you have to be able to forget the hurt they caused you. Also, in the forgiveness process, you have to be willing not to seek revenge on that person or people involved. 1 Corinthians13 (NLT) states: "Love is patient and kind. Love is not jealous or boastful or proud or rude. It doesn't demand its own way. Love never gives up, never loses faith is always hopeful and endures through every circumstance." If love is all these attributes, why did I feel alone, frustrated, hurt, mistreated, and unappreciated? How could he and I continue to call each other friends when we both felt disrespected?

Believing that God would surely bring me out, I remained faithful because I didn't want my children to see their mother emotionally scarred. Before I could attempt to teach my children, I wanted them to know that they were unique and very special. I wanted them to love themselves, to want to achieve greatness, and always have respect for all. Even though I was growing more frustrated with the situation I was in, I made sure to instill respect, honesty, and responsibility in my boys. No parent ever wants their child(ren) to watch as things go from bad to worse, so I hid my pain and put on a facade to make everyone comfortable in the house.

While in his apartment, so much went on where I needed to have a secret closet and a safe haven. Having people sleeping in the living room, nowhere to go to have peace of mind, clear my head, and every room filled with people definitely didn't help me find some normal in the madness I lived around. Sometimes I felt the most alone when the house was full of people who stayed there, and this was a concurrent wave of emotions daily. What was supposed to be a temporary stay turned into a two-year living arrangement that I desperately needed to get away from. Even though he and I were no longer together, we still lived in the same house and we decided we were going to respect one another's space, but somehow, he didn't adhere to these rules.

I respected that this was his house, but he also needed to understand that he couldn't treat me as though all

I was to him was the roommate. When I talked about leaving, he would always have an excuse for why I should stay and how I should wait a while and stack my money. All of this discouraged me from moving forward, from walking out the door into what should've been my breakthrough.

Just when I thought that things in this apartment were starting to be peaceful here comes an arrest warrant for him that took me by surprise. How was I supposed to explain this to impressionable boys who just saw cops taking away the man of the house? Why did this have to happen while my children were still there? Not only were my children and I there, but their father had just shown up as he was being escorted downstairs. What was I supposed to gain from being in this situation? I didn't understand it at the time, but I needed to see this man for who he was: a liar and someone who couldn't be trusted.

How was I going to respect him after this? I kept my mouth shut because I didn't know what to say to someone that obviously didn't care about how his decisions affected the house. Being here now, I was thrown into someone else's world to regain a clear perspective of who I was so I could be a great woman for myself and a mother to my children. What kind of man blamed others for his misdoings? There are some things in life that we all need to take responsibility and accountability for, such as: being locked up, being evicted, breakups, not being able to raise our children or losing ourselves. Every day I had the opportunity to learn and experience something new; it would be up to me to seize the opportunity.

It was going to be up to me to decide how my life was going to end up. I needed to make a crucial decision that I wanted more for my life as well as for my boys. I didn't deserve the treatment that I was getting since I was loyal to a man who was supposed to be my friend. A friend is someone who can see the truth and pain even when you're fooling everyone around you. Now that I was starting to see for myself what kind of person he really was, I made up my mind that I was worth more than the lies he told to soothe the situation he'd placed us in. How was I going to be able to live with him when he had no remorse for his actions? How could he live with himself knowing that he was dishonest, rude, disrespectful, and disobedient in his relationships with everyone around him?

Even though I still wasn't entirely comfortable in the house, I learned that I was way stronger for remaining in the apartment after that ordeal. At this point in my life, my strength and faith in God grew more daily because I was starting to gain power I didn't know I had. In gaining my inner strength, there was a maturity level that came with being mentally able to endure anything that happened after the arrest. What else could I withstand that I would have the courage to overcome? This would be the question of the year because I never imagined that my life would have been turned upside down from yet another family moving into what I called my home.

What I realized was that just because I paid rent didn't mean I could call this apartment my home.

The word DISRESPECT didn't enter the mind of my roommate when he decided he was going to move his new girlfriend and her son into the house. How the hell was this right? What was I going to tell my sons that now have to live with two people they didn't know? What went on in this man's mind to assume that I would be alright with the fact that I was his ex and now he was forcing me to share my living space. This was insane that here I was living with three people I didn't know and definitely didn't feel comfortable being around. I didn't know how the girlfriend felt, but I felt betrayed, completely disrespected, and disappointed that I had no say in the matter. I didn't care that she was the current flavor of the month; she needed to stay in her lane and respect the fact that I was in the house and I wasn't going to be pushed out by anyone.

Yes, I was angry and frustrated because I was paying all the bills in the house, so what was she doing there? I didn't know much about her except that she was 22, didn't work, and was there because she was having issues with her grandmother. From my experience being in the house with the two of them and discussing different things with them, neither he nor she had any clue to the realization of true life. They were clueless to the fact that life is going to happen every day and it's up to the people to either make corrections or fall by the wayside.

Every day was something different in the house that Jack built because dealing with my roommate; he still had it in his mind that what he was doing was right. How could he call himself a man when he had no regard for the people he was hurting? To make matters worse, my roommate decided to move his cousin into the living room with ease and yet again, no questions asked. I was getting to the point where I hated being in the house, and the people in it were becoming very annoying! No one besides me was working, paying bills, and buying food in the house, which eventually took a toll on me emotionally.

While getting frustrated, I started saying exactly what was on my mind and this would in turn create an argument that would come to blows with the roommate and me. Even with him and I having a physical altercation, he still thought that he could do what he wanted, which only made things worse in the house. I never thought that things between him and I would escalate to a fight and I was so apologetic to my boys for that because I didn't want them having the wrong impression of me. After the fight, I had a conversation with my boys so they could understand that I stood up for myself from a bully who disrespected me. How would I feel about myself if I allowed this so-called man to belittle me in front of my children? With his girlfriend's presence there showed me that he didn't have any respect for her either, so he was a pitiful person from this point on. No one should ever fear being in their home, but after that fight, I never wanted to be in the house, especially if I knew they were going to be there. However, being in the middle of their madness, I started to see that I was better than both of them and they had nothing going for themselves. Because they thought that I had no place to go, I decided that the best decision was for my sons and me to leave immediately.

I'm grateful for God's favor upon my life because he saved me from drowning in my misery in this apartment. No one will ever understand how sad I was every day and how I felt incomplete, lonely, frustrated, and mad that I had to go through this with my children. I know that we all have to go through hardships so that we could see God's hand at work, and I believe that I was made uncomfortable so that my faith could grow.

Due to this situation, I became mentally, spiritually, physically, and emotionally strong enough to handle anything that life may throw my way. I've learned so much about myself, having gone through that situation with strangers. No longer will I allow anyone to disrespect my children nor myself; no longer will I allow anyone to mistreat me because they think they can.

I have the power to overcome anything that may be thrown in my path of walking in my purpose. Courage comes from having faith. Faith comes by hearing and hearing by the word of God. God's word has always been my power source for striving to do better and it strengthens my character and my ability to be bold, brave, courageous, confident, effective, and fearless. For a long while, I was afraid that I would fail myself and my boys, but now that I'm trusting God there are a lot of things slowly turning around for me.

I don't know, nor do I need to know what Christ is going to do, but I'm grateful for everything that he's already done for me. The Bible states, "I can do all things through Christ who strengthens me" Philippians 4:13 (NKJV).

www.ingramcontent.com/pod-product-compliance
Lightning Source LLC
Chambersburg PA
CBHW051711090426
42736CB00013B/2640